Incorporation
of a North Carolina Town

David M. Lawrence
and
Kara A. Millonzi

Incorporation *of a* North Carolina Town

Third Edition 2007

UNC
SCHOOL OF GOVERNMENT

THE UNIVERSITY
of NORTH CAROLINA
at CHAPEL HILL

School of Government
University of North Carolina

The School of Government at the University of North Carolina at Chapel Hill works to improve the lives of North Carolinians by engaging in practical scholarship that helps public officials and citizens understand and strengthen state and local government. Established in 1931 as the Institute of Government, the School provides educational, advisory, and research services for state and local governments. The School of Government is also home to a nationally ranked graduate program in public administration and specialized centers focused on information technology, environmental finance, and civic education for youth.

As the largest university-based local government training, advisory, and research organization in the United States, the School of Government offers up to 200 classes, seminars, schools, and specialized conferences for more than 12,000 public officials each year. In addition, faculty members annually publish approximately fifty books, periodicals, and other reference works related to state and local government. Each day that the General Assembly is in session, the School produces the *Daily Bulletin*, which reports on the day's activities for members of the legislature and others who need to follow the course of legislation.

The Master of Public Administration Program is a full-time, two-year program that serves up to sixty students annually. It consistently ranks among the best public administration graduate programs in the country, particularly in city management. With courses ranging from public policy analysis to ethics and management, the program educates leaders for local, state, and federal governments and nonprofit organizations.

Operating support for the School of Government's programs and activities comes from many sources, including state appropriations, local government membership dues, private contributions, publication sales, course fees, and service contracts. Visit www.sog.unc.edu or call 919.966.5381 for more information on the School's courses, publications, programs, and services.

Michael R. Smith, Dean
Thomas H. Thornburg, Senior Associate Dean
Frayda S. Bluestein, Associate Dean for Programs
Todd A. Nicolet, Associate Dean for Information Technology
Ann Cary Simpson, Associate Dean for Development and Communications
Bradley G. Volk, Associate Dean for Administration

Faculty

Gregory S. Allison	Robert L. Farb	Janet Mason	Jessica Smith
Stephen Allred (on leave)	Joseph S. Ferrell	Laurie L. Mesibov	Karl W. Smith
David N. Ammons	Milton S. Heath Jr.	Kara A. Millonzi	Carl W. Stenberg III
A. Fleming Bell, II	Norma Houston (on leave)	Jill D. Moore	John B. Stephens
Maureen M. Berner	Cheryl Daniels Howell	Jonathan Q. Morgan	Charles A. Szypszak
Mark F. Botts	Joseph E. Hunt	Ricardo S. Morse	Vaughn Upshaw
Joan G. Brannon	Willow S. Jacobson	David W. Owens	A. John Vogt
Molly C. Broad	Robert P. Joyce	William C. Rivenbark	Aimee N. Wall
Michael Crowell	Diane M. Juffras	Dale J. Roenigk	Richard B. Whisnant
Shea Riggsbee Denning	David M. Lawrence	John Rubin	Gordon P. Whitaker
James C. Drennan	Dona G. Lewandowski	John L. Saxon	Eileen Youens
Richard D. Ducker	James M. Markham	Shannon H. Schelin	

Contents

Preface

This guide is intended for persons interested in incorporating a town in North Carolina. It discusses the reasons communities incorporate, some alternatives to incorporation, the processes of incorporation, and what it means to be a town. It also considers the problems of financing a newly incorporated town, sets out three sample budgets to assist in understanding the cost of town services and the resources available to meet them, and suggests some of the initial steps local officials must take once a town has been incorporated.

The guide is based largely on the experiences of various School of Government faculty members who over several decades have advised communities interested in incorporation. Officials in several towns incorporated during the last decade have also discussed with us some of the issues faced by their towns. We are grateful for their insights.

David M. Lawrence
William Rand Kenan Jr. Professor of
 Public Law and Government

Kara A. Millonzi
Assistant Professor of Public Law and
 Government

1. Why Incorporate?

A community incorporates as a town because its citizens want one or more of the advantages that accompany town government.[1] One such advantage is the ability to provide residents the entire range of urban services associated with city and town government: police and fire protection, street maintenance, solid waste collection and disposal, water and sewer services, recreation facilities, and so on. North Carolina law *permits* every town to provide the full range of city services—a town of 400 population has the same powers under the North Carolina General Statutes as the city of Charlotte—but the law does not *require* that each city or town provide all services. Each town, through its elected governing board, decides which services it will provide.

A second advantage of incorporation is a town's ability to regulate its citizens and their property through ordinance-making power. Among the most common ordinances are those that zone property, control dogs and other animals, limit commercial solicitation, and restrict the use of firearms.

Third, incorporation forecloses the possibility that a community will be annexed by an existing, neighboring city or town. No city may annex territory that is within another city or town.

---

1. In North Carolina an incorporated municipality may be called a *town*, a *city*, or a *village*, as it chooses. The terms are completely interchangeable. In this booklet the term generally used is *town*, because it is the choice of most smaller municipalities.

Finally, incorporation brings with it a variety of other rights. For example, a town is eligible to receive certain federal or state grants or loans not available to an unincorporated community. Also, a town having at least 500 residents and located in a dry county may vote to permit beer or wine sales; and a town having at least 500 registered voters (in a few cases, 300 registered voters) may vote to establish Alcoholic Beverage Control (ABC) stores or permit the sale of mixed beverages.

Of course the benefits of incorporation do not come without costs—costs directly related to the benefits. First, it costs money to provide town services, and some of that money normally must be provided by taxation. While many residents of a community might view the additional layer of taxation as compensation for the new services, not everyone does. Further, town regulations that are welcomed by some may be viewed by others as unnecessary encroachments on their freedom. For example, dog owners may have a different view of a dog-control ordinance than their neighbors do.

Citizens who are considering incorporating their community must weigh the advantages and disadvantages as they apply to the particular circumstances of that community. How serious is the need for new services? How much will those services cost? Are there alternative ways of getting the services? Will zoning be a protection against bad choices by neighbors or an undesirable restriction on property rights? How likely is annexation by a nearby city in the near future? The answers will differ from community to community and from person to person, as a review of incorporation votes over the past several decades will demonstrate.

2. Alternatives to Incorporation

If citizens of a community want to avoid annexation or hold a liquor election, they must incorporate; only incorporation enables them to achieve these goals. If, however, they merely want to secure one or more municipal services or implement some form of governmental regulation, there are alternatives to incorporation: for example, provision of services or enactment of regulations by the county, creation of one or another sort of taxing or special district, or annexation by a nearby city or town. These alternatives are discussed in this chapter.

The County

A county is authorized to provide almost all the major services that a town may provide, with the exception of street and sidewalk construction and maintenance. A county may also adopt essentially the same range of ordinances as a town may. Thus, except for street and sidewalk services, the county in which a community is located may legally provide for all the community's service and regulatory needs.

Not all counties provide urban services, however, and of those that do, not all maintain them at the level that a particular community might desire. Similarly, not all counties exercise the regulatory powers they enjoy; as of 2006, for example, twenty-five counties still did no zoning. Even when a county does undertake regulatory programs, its commissioners are responsible to the entire county rather than to the residents of a particular community within it. Thus, when the service and regulatory needs of one community differ significantly from those of the rest of the county, it may be necessary to establish a governmental entity that is specifically limited to that community.

County Service Districts

One such entity is the *county service district*. This is an area within a county whose boundaries are set by the board of county commissioners. The county levies a tax on property within the district, in addition to the countywide property tax, and uses the additional proceeds to provide one or more services that it either does not provide countywide or does not provide at as high a level as residents of the district desire. Providing a service through such a district may permit the county to realize economies of scale that would not be available to a newly incorporated small town.

Service districts, however, are not available for the full range of municipal services. The statutes permit a county to establish such a district to provide one or more of the following services:

- water supply and distribution
- sewage collection and disposal
- fire protection
- solid waste collection and disposal
- ambulance and rescue squad
- recreation
- watershed improvement
- beach erosion control
- cemeteries

Notably missing from the list are street and sidewalk construction and maintenance, which a county cannot provide at all, and (with one exception) police protection.[1]

Establishing a service district is entirely within the discretion of the board of county commissioners. District residents need not petition the commissioners, and no referendum of district residents on establishing the district is required, or even authorized. In addition, once a district has been established, decisions about the level of service provided are made by the county commissioners. A separate board composed of district residents is not required, although the commissioners can appoint an advisory committee of such residents if they find it useful. Thus, although service districts generally are not established unless desired by district residents, control over policy making for such districts rests solely with the board of county commissioners.

Special Districts

Three types of special districts—limited-purpose local government units that provide specific urban services—also are possible under North Carolina law. The special district that most resembles a town is the *sanitary district*, which is authorized to provide the following services:

- water supply and distribution
- sewage collection and disposal
- solid waste collection and disposal
- fire protection
- maintenance of roads not up to state standards
- cemeteries

---

1. The county service district statute, N.C. Gen. Stat. 153A-301(b) and (c) (hereinafter G.S.), does permit a coastal-area county to establish a service district for either removal of junk automobiles or street maintenance. G.S. 153A-301(a)(10) permits Mecklenburg County to establish a service district to pay for police protection provided under a service contract by the city of Charlotte. No other counties enjoy this authority.

But a sanitary district has no authority to provide law enforcement, and it has only a very limited ordinance-making power.[2]

A sanitary district is established jointly by the State Commission for Health Services and the board of commissioners of the county within which the district (or the greater part of its area) lies, upon receipt of a petition from residents of the proposed district. Because the petition must include the signatures of more than half the property owners, it is not particularly easy to obtain. Once a sanitary district is established, the county commissioners appoint the original district board; thereafter the district's voters elect board members. Currently there are thirty-nine sanitary districts in North Carolina.

Two other types of special districts have more limited purposes. A *rural fire protection district*, which is established by the appropriate board of county commissioners after approval by district voters, may finance fire protection as well as ambulance, rescue, and emergency medical services. Although the county commissioners may establish a fire commission for a rural fire protection district, they retain the district's tax-levying power.

The third sort of special district is the *county water and sewer district*, which is created by the board of county commissioners to provide water, sewer, or both. The commissioners establish such a district on their own initiative and action and automatically serve as the district's governing board.

Annexation

The final alternative to incorporation for communities that wish to obtain urban services is annexation by a nearby city or town. As a practical matter, this alternative is feasible only if the unincorporated community is adjacent to the city or town and is sufficiently urbanized to meet the annexation statutes' definitions of urban development. In addition, the decision about whether to annex an area rests entirely with the existing city or town. If annexed, the community becomes entitled to all services provided by the city or town, subject to all its regulations, and liable for the payment of all its taxes.

---

2. Sanitary districts that meet certain criteria set out in G.S. 130A-55(17) are permitted to adopt zoning ordinances, but at the time of publication only one district had met the criteria.

3. How to Incorporate

Legal Procedures

Approval by the General Assembly

Under current North Carolina law, a town may be incorporated only by act of the General Assembly. The decision to incorporate a community is essentially a political one; the General Assembly is not bound by any standards of population density, development, or tax base. It may incorporate an area with only a few residents or with a largely rural character; it may even incorporate an area in anticipation of development, before any sort of town actually exists. A state constitutional provision does, however, require that certain incorporations be approved by a larger than normal majority within the legislature. Article VII, section 1, of the state constitution directs that if a community lies within one mile of the limits of an existing city with a population of 5,000 or more, within three miles of a city of 10,000 or more, within four miles of a city of 25,000 or more, or within five miles of a city of 50,000 or more, the General Assembly may incorporate that community only with the approval of three-fifths of the members of each legislative house.

Joint Legislative Commission on Municipal Incorporations

In most instances the General Assembly seeks the advice of the Joint Legislative Commission on Municipal Incorporations (the Joint Commission) established under Chapter 120, Article 20, of the North Carolina General Statutes (hereinafter G.S.). During the first decade after its establishment in 1986, the commission was little used by the General Assembly. Since about 1997, however, legislators have required that almost all incorporation proposals be submitted to and reviewed by the Joint Commission; proponents of an incorporation should therefore expect to follow the Joint Commission's procedures. For the commission to have jurisdiction to review a proposed incorporation, it must receive, at least sixty days before the next regular legislative session, a petition signed by at least 15 percent of the registered voters in the area proposed for incorporation. The statute directs the commission to consider the proposed town's proximity to existing cities or towns, its population, the nature and degree of development within the proposed town, the proposed package of municipal services to be provided by the town, and whether it will be able to provide those services at a reasonable tax rate. At the conclusion of its investigation the Joint Commission makes either a positive or negative recommendation to the General Assembly. It cannot make a positive recommendation for incorporation unless all of the following requirements are met:

- Each existing city or town close enough to the proposed town to require a three-fifths vote for incorporation by the General Assembly has expressly approved the incorporation.
- The proposed town has a permanent population of at least 100 and a permanent or seasonal population density of at least 250 persons per square mile.
- At least 40 percent of the area of the proposed town is in urban development.
- The proponents have submitted to the Joint Commission with their petition a plan for levying a tax rate of at least 5 cents per $100 valuation and, by the third year following incorporation, for providing at least four of the following eight municipal services: police protection, fire protection, solid waste collection or disposal, water distribution, street maintenance, street construction or right-of-way acquisition, street lighting, and zoning.
- The commission has determined that the proposed town will be able to provide the services requested in the petition by levying a reasonable tax rate.

If the commission cannot make a positive recommendation, the statute requires that it make a negative recommendation. Although a negative recommendation often ends an incorporation effort, the General Assembly is free to incorporate a community receiving such a recommendation. It has occasionally done just that.[1]

Voter Approval

When the General Assembly incorporates a community, it may either make the incorporation effective immediately or first require that the area's residents approve it in a referendum. The decision on whether to require voter approval rests solely with the General Assembly; local voters have no inherent constitutional right to vote on an incorporation. (If the legislature calls for a referendum, all fund-raising activities and advertising for the referendum are subject to the limitations and reporting requirements set out in G.S. Chapter 163, Article 22A.)

The Federal Voting Rights Act

Forty North Carolina counties are subject to Section 5 of the federal Voting Rights Act, which protects the voting rights of minorities by requiring that the U.S. attorney general approve any incorporation legislation in those counties. A community's representatives in the General Assembly can determine whether the county in which the proposed town is located is covered by the statute; if it is, the county attorney is responsible for seeking the necessary federal approval. No North Carolina incorporation has failed to be approved under this procedure, but the requirement to obtain federal approval could delay a referendum or, if no referendum is called, the effective date of incorporation.

---

1. At one time the Senate's rules required a proposed incorporation to be submitted to the commission before being considered by the Senate, but they no longer do so. Each house of the General Assembly does require that the commission's recommendations, if any, be attached to the incorporation bill, but that is all.

Contacting Legislators

At an early date, leaders of a community that wishes to incorporate should get in touch with the legislators who represent their community in the General Assembly. Those legislators can advise the community about whether it will need to submit the proposal to the Joint Commission and whether those legislators will agree to introduce and support passage of an incorporation bill. If they do, the legislation should pass with no difficulty, even if a three-fifths vote is necessary under the constitutional requirement mentioned above.

Practical Concerns

Before submitting a petition asking the Joint Commission or the General Assembly to consider an incorporation bill, backers of the proposal need to organize and make a few important policy decisions about the proposed new town and its government and gather information that may be important to citizens, the Joint Commission, or legislators. This entire process will usually take at least six months and may extend for more than a year.

First, the backers must organize themselves to provide oversight and management of the incorporation effort. Sometimes an existing community organization can assume that role; sometimes the coordinating group will have to be created, often self-created by those citizens most interested in incorporation. (In the rest of this chapter this group will be referred to as *the proponents*.)

Second, the proponents need to set tentative town boundaries so that individual property owners know whether their property is to be included in the proposed town. This step leads to meeting two further requirements for incorporation: a map of the proposed town to accompany the petition submitted to the Joint Commission and a legal description of the proposed boundaries to include in the legislation incorporating the town. With respect to this final requirement, it should be noted that the General Assembly's drafting office strongly prefers to receive some sort of metes and bounds description of the town's boundaries. Such a description can be prepared by a surveyor; it can also be prepared by using the county's tax-mapping system. (These initial boundaries can be adjusted throughout the process if that seems advisable.)

Third, once the initial boundaries are set, the total value of taxable property within the proposed town should be determined. This information is essential to estimating the financial implications of incorporation. The county tax assessor's office can supply these figures.

Fourth, the proponents should interview county officials—the manager, planning director, and finance officer—to (1) determine what the county is now doing in the area of the proposed town and what it plans to do and (2) become familiar with any relevant county studies on land use, utilities, topography, and the like.

Fifth, the act incorporating the town will include the town's charter. This document sets out the town boundaries and establishes the size, terms of office, and method of election of the town's governing board and mayor. In addition, the petition submitted to the Joint Commission must include this information about the governing board and mayor. Several options are possible concerning how the board will be structured and the mayor selected.[2] The coordinating group normally makes the choices among possible charter provisions, which are then included in the petition and forwarded to the General Assembly's drafting office.

Sixth, if the incorporation is to be submitted to the Joint Commission, the proponents must organize the process of obtaining the necessary signatures on the incorporation petition and make sure that they have the other information the commission requires.

Seventh, the community's residents usually want to know how much a town government will cost, especially what the property tax rate is likely to be and what services they will receive. As noted above, an incorporation proposal that is submitted to the Joint Commission must include a plan for providing at least four of the eight services listed. Therefore, proponents usually find it useful to develop a model budget for the town. The sample budgets set

---

2. Appendix A sets out the current pattern of governing board structures in North Carolina; Appendix B. contains a model town charter.

out in Chapter 5, "Financing a Town," should help those developing such a model. Visits or calls to existing towns of roughly the same size are usually very helpful.

In addition, proponents can gather information residents will want about the agencies, public and private, that are currently providing services in the community. How do the costs and levels of service provided by those agencies compare with the costs and proposed town services shown in the proposed budget?

Finally, proponents—and legislators—will want to know what others in the community think of incorporation. The petitions required for submission to the Joint Commission are one way to gauge community sentiment, but other methods have been used as well. Community meetings—often in a local school or other public facility—can be convened to explain incorporation, answer questions, and obtain responses. A more ambitious process would be a house-to-house survey to document community needs and citizens' thoughts on incorporation.

Two, or possibly three, agencies can help a community that is interested in incorporating. They are the School of Government at the University of North Carolina at Chapel Hill; the North Carolina League of Municipalities, a voluntary organization of the state's cities and towns; and, sometimes, the seventeen councils of governments—regional organizations of counties, cities, and towns.

4. The Opportunities and Responsibilities of Incorporation

What does it mean to be a town? What services must or may a town provide? What sorts of ordinances can it adopt? What other effects does incorporation have? This chapter presents a brief discussion of town services, town regulatory power, and the choices available to towns under the state liquor laws.

Town Services—What Is Required?

There is considerable confusion over whether newly incorporated towns are required to provide a minimum number of services and what those services might be. Three separate statutes contribute to that confusion.

One Absolutely Mandated Service

There is only one service that state law requires each city and town to either provide or arrange for some other government to provide: enforcement of the State Building Code. Most small towns meet this requirement by contracting with the county government or a nearby large city to conduct the necessary inspections; therefore, as a practical matter, small towns are not *required* to provide any services at all.

Plans for Four Services Submitted to the Joint Commission

When a new town proposal is submitted to the Joint Legislative Commission on Municipal Incorporations (Joint Commission), the commission may not make a positive recommendation to incorporate the town unless petitioners submit a plan for (a) offering at least four municipal services from a list of eight by the third year of incorporation and (b) levying a property tax of at least 5 cents per $100 valuation.[1] The eight services from which the petitioners may choose are

- police protection
- fire protection
- solid waste collection or disposal
- water distribution
- street maintenance
- street construction or right-of-way acquisition
- street lighting
- zoning

It should be noted, however, that a plan submitted by persons who later might or might not be empowered to make decisions on behalf of the incorporated town is not legally binding; only the eventual town governing body will have legal power to make decisions about which services to provide. The plan submitted to the Joint Commission simply satisfies a condition that must be met to achieve the commission's positive recommendation.

Conditions for Receiving Certain State-Collected Revenues

To receive the state-collected revenues listed below a town incorporated after 1999 must include in its annual budget appropriations for at least four of the same statutory list of eight services set out just above.[2] In addition, the town must levy a property tax of at least

---

1. N.C. GEN. STAT. 120-163(c), 120-169.1(b) (hereinafter G.S.).
2. The basic requirement is set out in G.S. 136-41.2(c), which deals with state street assistance; this section is then cross-referenced in the particular legislation associated with each of the other affected revenues.

five cents and must open a majority of the town's street mileage to the general public. The affected revenues are

- local government sales and use taxes
- state street assistance (Powell Bill moneys)
- state beer and wine tax proceeds
- state electric utility franchise tax proceeds
- state telecommunications tax proceeds
- video programming tax proceeds

It should be noted that a town incorporated after 1999 must meet these requirements every year to receive the listed revenues; it does not have three years in which to meet them, as it does for the plan required in the Joint Commission submission.

As most new towns wish to receive the listed revenues, this condition operates, in practice, as a requirement to provide at least four services and levy a property tax of at least five cents. But not all new towns are willing to levy the five-cent tax rate and provide the four services. If a town is willing to forgo the state-collected revenues, it need not meet the condition.

Town Services—The Usual Mix

Most cities and towns in North Carolina, including most newly incorporated towns, provide some or all of a set of core services. This section briefly considers each of these basic services.

Streets

The public roads in an unincorporated community are maintained by the state Department of Transportation (DOT). Once a community is incorporated, its officials sit down with DOT's district engineer to decide which of the town's public roads will become town streets and which will remain the state's responsibility. (This agreement is confirmed by action of both the town governing board and the N.C. Board of Transportation.) The state normally retains charge of all through highways plus roads that lead to major destinations within the town; all others normally become the town's responsibility. (A few newly incorporated towns have chosen not to assume any street maintenance at all. In these towns, DOT remains responsible for all street maintenance, paying for it with the money available for maintaining secondary roads generally. A town without responsibility for its streets receives no Powell Bill moneys.)

Once a town accepts responsibility for its streets, it becomes eligible for a share of the street aid distributed by the state.[3] Smaller towns often contract with DOT for assistance in maintaining town streets, using the state street aid money as payment. Many towns, however, find that adequately maintaining town streets requires them to supplement state money with town-raised funds.

There are currently three incorporated towns in North Carolina in which most streets are behind gates and open only to town residents and their guests. Occasionally other gated communities consider incorporation. Although state policy does not prohibit incorporation of more gated communities, it does discourage it. As noted above, if a town wants to receive the various state-collected revenues listed above (except for state street aid), it must open a majority of the town's street mileage to the general public. Thus, a mostly gated community that incorporates and wishes to retain its gates will forgo all the listed state-collected revenues except state street assistance. Even with respect to the street distribution, the gated town will only receive revenue for its ungated street mileage.

Law Enforcement

Sheriff's departments usually do not provide law enforcement within incorporated towns, expecting that the towns will have their own police departments. (Occasionally a sheriff does continue to patrol in small towns, often under a contract with the town. This is sometimes a transitional arrangement for a newly incorporated town.) Most towns employ one or more

---

3. See discussion of motor fuels tax below in Chapter 5, "Financing a Town."

police officers who, by state mandate, must meet the training and certification requirements of the state's Criminal Justice Training and Standards Council.

Fire Protection

Most small communities are served by volunteer fire departments, and incorporation normally has no effect on this service arrangement. The payment arrangements may change, however. If the community is part of a rural fire protection district or a county service district for fire protection, incorporation does not automatically remove the community from the district. The new town, however, often withdraws from the district so that it can levy its own tax for fire protection in lieu of the district tax. This enables the town to count fire protection as one of the four services required to receive state-collected revenues.

Water and Sewer Services

If a community water or sewer system is already in place, the new town may choose to make no changes. But if the system is privately owned, the operator may prefer the town to assume control and sometimes deeds the system to the town for a nominal amount.

If no community water or sewer system exists and the town wants to construct such a system, it normally has to borrow the money to do so, stretching out the repayment period for as long as forty years. These systems, especially sewer systems, are very expensive, and most new towns do not embark upon such a project for some time. Occasionally a new town is able to contract with a nearby city or with the county for water supply or sewage treatment and disposal, thereby reducing significantly the capital costs of the system. Another possibility is contracting with a nearby local government to extend its water or sewer lines to properties in the new town.

Solid Waste

When a new town decides to provide solid waste collection for its residents, it frequently finds it convenient to enter into a contract with a private collector, thus avoiding the need to purchase expensive collection vehicles.

A town that wants to provide solid waste collection—either with town employees or by contracting with a private collector—will have to either compensate existing private collectors who have been providing service within the town or delay implementing its arrangements for more than a year. Under G.S. 160A-327, when a local government displaces an existing solid waste collection firm by providing competing services financed with taxation, the local government must either wait fifteen months before beginning its competing service or pay the displaced private firm an amount equal to the revenues the firm received in the last six months it provided service in the town's area.

Street Lighting

If a new town decides to pay the cost of street lights within the town, it is a simple matter to contract with the local electric power company for installation and operation of the lighting equipment.

Town Regulatory Powers

Each town in North Carolina has full authority to adopt ordinances regulating activities within its borders. This authority includes the power to divide the town into zones and to regulate land use within each zone. In addition, if the county does not zone land, regulate subdivisions, and enforce the State Building Code in the area just outside a town, the town may exercise its zoning power up to one mile beyond the town limits in all directions.[4] This extraterritorial jurisdiction (ETJ) also extends to other development regulations, such as subdivision controls, housing code enforcement, and control of historic properties.

If the county *is* exercising zoning, subdivision, and inspection powers just outside the town, the town's capacity to regulate development is limited to its own territory unless the county agrees to cede ETJ to the town. Alternatively, the town may reach an agreement with

4. G.S. 160A-360.

the county to give the latter responsibility for these development regulations within the town as well.

If a county does regulate development in the area of a new town—usually through zoning—the county's regulations stay in effect until the new town adopts its own regulations or for sixty days, whichever period is *shorter*. If the town does not adopt zoning regulations within that sixty-day period, no zoning will be in effect in the new town until it does so. Other county ordinances also cease to be in effect within a town on the effective date of its incorporation.

Subdivision Covenants

In recent years many proposed incorporations have included subdivision developments. Residents of such developments often wonder how incorporation will affect the covenants that apply to their properties. Such covenants may include land-use limitations, requirements for homeowners' association approval of changes to houses or yards, or liability for homeowners' association assessments. Incorporation has no effect on such covenants: they remain in effect, along with any comparable land-use regulations and property taxes adopted by the new town's governing board. Of course, if the town assumes responsibility for some of the community services formerly provided by the homeowners' association, assessments for those services may decrease.

Liquor Laws

Under state law, a town with 500 or more residents, or 500 or more registered voters, is authorized to hold elections about alcoholic beverage control. For example, if the sale of beer or wine is not legal in the county, a town in that county with at least 500 residents may hold a referendum on whether to permit the sale of malt beverages, wine, or both.[5] In addition, a

---

5. G.S. 18B-600(c).

town with at least 500 registered voters in a county that does not have a countywide system of state-regulated Alcoholic Beverage Control (ABC) stores may hold a referendum on establishing a town ABC system.[6] Finally, if a town with at least 500 registered voters has an ABC system, or is located in a county that has an ABC system but does not permit the sale of mixed beverages, it may hold a referendum on whether to permit the sale of mixed beverages within the town.[7]

Town Procedural Requirements

When a community incorporates, the new town and its governing board become subject to a variety of statutes that impose procedural requirements on the conduct of town business. These statutes typically create rules that are unique to government, so that board members and employees who come from the private sector might not always anticipate them. Some examples of these special requirements include

- the open meetings law
- various public records statutes
- governmental procurement and contracting requirements
- conflict-of-interest prohibitions
- budgeting and financial administration requirements
- record retention requirements

A new town should rely on its town attorney to help the governing board and town employees navigate these special requirements as they apply to local government operations.

---

6. G.S. 18B-600(d).

7. G.S. 18B-600(e).

5. Financing a Town

A major responsibility of a newly incorporated town is obtaining sufficient revenue to cover the costs of the services it wishes to provide. Some new towns choose to provide the bare minimum in services. These towns often assess a property tax of 5 cents per $100 valuation but impose few other local taxes or fees. (Although the five-cent rate might seem arbitrary, it is actually the minimum rate required to tap into many county- and state-shared revenue sources). Other new towns incorporate for the very purpose of providing more extensive services to their citizens. These towns need to understand the full range of revenue-raising mechanisms that are available to fund those services.

This chapter summarizes the principal revenue sources available to an incorporated town, details the mechanics of raising the revenue, identifies relevant eligibility requirements, and describes any restrictions on the use of the proceeds. It then provides reference information helpful for estimating the revenue a new town can expect to receive from each potential source. Finally, it sets forth three sample budgets, based on different population sizes, to give communities a sense of revenues and expenditures expected.

Principal Revenue Sources

Locally Raised Revenue

Property tax. The property tax, also known as the ad valorem tax, is the primary locally raised revenue source for many cities, towns, and counties in North Carolina. It is levied against *real property*, such as land, buildings, and other improvements to land; against *personal property*, such as business equipment and automobiles; and against the *property of public service companies*. Although a town sets its own tax rate, both the General Assembly and the county in which the town is located affect the amount a town can raise through property taxation. The General Assembly classifies property for purposes of taxation and provides for a number of exemptions and exclusions from the property tax base.[1] By constitutional mandate, the classifications, exclusions, and exemptions must be uniform across the state and cannot vary by county, city, or other geographic distinction. No town can exempt, classify, or otherwise give a property within its jurisdiction a tax preference. The authority to determine the tax value of all taxable property within the town lies with the county, and the town must accept its valuations. The town then levies a tax, when the annual budget is adopted, against the tax-base valuation. With one exception, the state constitution requires that all property in the town be taxed at a uniform rate.[2]

To set the rate, the town's governing board must first determine its total anticipated expenditures for the upcoming fiscal year; it then subtracts the total of anticipated revenue from all other sources—other local taxes, fees, and shared revenues from the county and state—from the figure for anticipated expenditures. Because North Carolina law requires all local governments to operate under a balanced budget, the difference between anticipated expenditures and anticipated revenues from all other sources must be raised through property taxation. The tax rate is calculated by dividing the total amount that needs to be raised by property taxation by the expected collection rate. The resulting figure is then divided by the total taxable valuation of the town and multiplied by 100 to produce the tax rate per $100 valuation. The collection rate reflects the amount of actual property tax revenue the town expects to collect during the fiscal year. It typically ranges from 95 to 99 percent. For its first budget year, a new town is advised to use the county's collection rate

---

1. The state constitution explicitly exempts certain properties from taxation; for example, under Article V, Sections 2(2) and (3), government-owned property is exempt from property taxation.

2. Article V, Section 2(4) of the state constitution authorizes the General Assembly to permit a town to define certain areas within its borders as special service districts and to levy additional taxes in those areas to provide certain specified services or facilities that are either not offered throughout the unit or are offered at a lower level.

from the prior fiscal year, although it is not required to use this rate. In subsequent budget years, the town may not calculate the tax rate by using a collection rate higher than its actual collection rate in the preceding fiscal year.

To illustrate the calculation, assume that a town must collect $200,000 in property tax revenue to balance its budget and that it expects to collect 96 percent of the property tax levy. To calculate the property tax rate, divide $200,000 by .96 to yield $208,333 as the total levy required. Next, divide the total levy by the town's total taxable valuation—say, $60 million—which yields approximately .0035. Finally, multiply the resulting figure by 100 to get a tax rate of $.35 per $100 valuation.

The town levies the tax when the annual budget is adopted in June or July against the valuation certified to it by the county. If a town is established by the General Assembly after the beginning of a fiscal year, the town's initial charter normally permits it to adopt a budget and levy taxes for the remainder of that first year. The town may collect its own tax levy, but because of the complicated nature of tax collections, most towns contract with the county to collect property taxes. Property taxes are due on September 1 of each year, but taxpayers may delay payment without penalty until January 5. Thus, as a practical matter, a town should expect to receive most of its property tax revenue in the middle of the fiscal year.

The General Assembly indirectly limits the purposes for which property tax proceeds may be spent by establishing an outer limit on the total property tax rate that a town can assess to fund most activities.

Motor vehicle license tax. Another local tax typically imposed by a new town is the motor vehicle license tax. Pursuant to general legislative authority, a city or town may levy a tax of up to $5.00 per year on any vehicle that is kept in the town. The proceeds from the tax may be used to fund any activity in which a town is authorized to engage. Additionally, if a town operates a public transportation system, it may levy an extra tax of up to $5.00 per year. The proceeds from the extra $5.00 tax, however, are earmarked for public transportation expenditures only. Finally, a city or town may assess up to $15 per year on each vehicle operated within its territory as a taxicab. Although widely used by most municipalities across the state, the motor vehicle license tax is a relatively minor source of income.

Other local taxes. There are several other (relatively minor) local taxes a town has general authority to levy. The use of these revenue-raising mechanisms and the amount of revenue they generate vary—depending on a range of local factors. The taxes include *privilege license taxes*, which are imposed on certain businesses, occupations, trades, employment, or activities; *animal taxes*, levied on the privilege of keeping dogs and other pets in the town; *franchise taxes*, assessed on airports, ambulance companies, off-street parking facilities, solid waste collection and disposal companies, taxicab companies, and private water and sewer service providers; *rental car gross-receipts taxes* levied on car rental companies operating inside the town; and certain charges for 911 services. Except for 911 service charges, the revenue from these taxes can be used to fund any activity in which a town is authorized to engage.

Several towns across the state also have the authority to assess occupancy taxes, prepared-food taxes, and local real estate transfer taxes. As there is no general authority to levy these taxes, a town must seek special local legislation from the General Assembly. Because of the political compromises necessary to ensure passage of local legislation, authorizations for these additional taxes often specifically restrict or earmark the use of the revenues they produce.

Fees and charges. A town can assess its citizens a variety of fees, most of them tied directly to specific services or facilities the town provides. Many towns charge user fees for General Fund services such as recreation or cultural programs, ambulance services, or cemetery lots. Several towns, including some small towns, also own and operate public enterprises to provide water, sewer, and solid waste collection services. With some restrictions, a town can impose fees for the use of these services—including impact or capacity fees, connection charges, monthly fixed and variable charges, penalties, and, under certain circumstances, availability fees. In fact, many towns strive to make these services self-supporting through the various user fees.

In addition to user fees, a town can impose fees or charges for the regulatory activities that it performs. The fees or charges must be reasonable—that is, roughly related to the cost of the activity performed. For example, a town may assess permit or inspection fees pursuant to its power to enforce building codes.

Finally, a town may levy special assessments against certain property for public improvements to streets, sidewalks, water systems, sewage systems, storm sewer and drainage systems and for beach erosion and flood and hurricane protection projects that benefit the properties assessed. A detailed statutory scheme governing special assessments includes a requirement that the assessments not be levied until the improvement being financed has been completed—a constraint that limits the number of small towns using them.

County and State Shared Revenues

Local option sales and use taxes. Often the largest percentage of total revenue for North Carolina cities and towns—aside from property tax proceeds and, for some towns, public enterprise fees—comes from local-option sales and use tax proceeds. There are in fact two types of local option sales and use taxes. The *sales tax* is a tax on the rental, sale, or lease of tangible personal property and on the rental of hotel rooms. The *use tax* is an excise tax on the right to use or consume property in North Carolina. Currently the General Assembly authorizes counties (not cities or towns) to levy four different sales and use taxes—totaling 2.5 percent—and all one hundred counties levy the full amount authorized.

The local sales and use taxes are collected by the state, and the net proceeds are distributed among the hundred counties on a monthly basis according to specified allocation formulas. Sales tax revenues are shared by each county with its eligible cities and towns according to one of two formulas based on either relative property tax levies or relative populations of the local government units located in the county. The board of county commissioners determines which method will be used.

As part of a comprehensive Medicaid relief package adopted by the state legislature during the 2007 regular session, counties will cede their authority to levy 0.50 percent of the local sales and use taxes over the next two years: 0.25 percent as of October 1, 2008, and an additional 0.25 percent as of October 1, 2009. Counties will reimburse cities incorporated on or before October 1, 2008, for the lost revenue roughly equivalent to the proceeds of 0.50 percent of the local sales and use taxes. Cities incorporated after that date will receive a distribution of only 2 percent of the local sales and use taxes.[3]

---

3. S.L. 2007-323.

How soon a new town receives its monthly allocation depends on how the revenues are distributed. If distribution is based on population, the town will receive its first check following the first full calendar month after incorporation. If, however, distribution is based on its tax levy, the town will have to wait a long while for its first sales and use tax check. Distribution under this method is based on the tax levy of the immediately preceding year; therefore, the town will not receive its check until the second year in which it has levied a property tax.

Furthermore, to receive the local sales and use tax distribution, a town must meet five eligibility requirements.

1. It must have conducted the most recent municipal elections required by its charter, or general law.
2. It must have levied a property tax for the current fiscal year of at least 5 cents per $100 valuation on all taxable property within its corporate limits and, except for the first year, have actually collected at least 50 percent of the total tax levied for the preceding fiscal year.
3. It must have formally adopted a budget ordinance that is in substantial compliance with applicable law.
4. It must have appropriated funds for at least four of the following eight municipal services: police protection, fire protection, solid waste collection or disposal, water distribution, street maintenance, street construction or right-of-way acquisition, street lighting, and zoning.
5. A majority of its street mileage must be open to the public.

A town may use its local sales and use tax proceeds to fund any activity in which a town is authorized to engage.

Motor fuels tax (Powell Bill funds). As noted in Chapter 4, "The Opportunities and Responsibilities of Incorporation," when a town is incorporated, its governing board will work with the state Department of Transportation (NCDOT) to determine what streets will be maintained by the town. Under certain circumstances, the town will be eligible to receive state funds (known as Powell Bill funds) to support its maintenance of public streets.

The proceeds from a state retail excise tax on gasoline sales (1.75 cents per gallon), along with 6.5 percent of the net proceeds of the North Carolina Highway Trust Fund, also are distributed annually to eligible cities and towns. Three-quarters of the proceeds are distributed among the towns based on their relative populations, and one-quarter is distributed according to the relative number of miles of non-state streets in each town.

To receive the Powell Bill funds, a town must meet the same eligibility requirements as it does to receive local sales and use tax proceeds, except that a majority of the town's street mileage does not have to be open to the public. Expenditure of Powell Bill funds, though, is limited to public streets.

A town that is incorporated on or before July 1 of a given fiscal year and otherwise complies with the eligibility requirements will receive its first annual allocation of Powell Bill funds on or before October 1 of that year. Otherwise, it will receive the allocation on or before October 1 of the following fiscal year.

A town may use its Powell Bill funds to maintain, repair, and construct public streets or thoroughfares, including bridges, drainage, curbs and gutters, and other necessary appurtenances of public streets, including sidewalks. The North Carolina Department of Revenue has a detailed list of what expenditures are and are not allowed.[4]

Electric franchise tax. Quarterly, the state shares with each eligible city and town the proceeds from a tax of approximately 3.09 percent on the gross receipts derived by an electric power company from sales within the city or town.

To receive the electric franchise tax funds, a town must meet the same eligibility requirements as it does to receive the local sales and use tax proceeds. A town may use its electric franchise tax proceeds to fund any activity in which a town is authorized to engage.

---

4. For a list of authorized Powell Bill fund expenditures as of 2006, see http://www.nctreasurer.com/LGC/ compsup2006/state/DOT-4-2006.pdf (last visited 20 June 2007).

A new town should receive its first quarterly share of the electric franchise tax proceeds within seventy-five days of the end of the first calendar quarter after it is incorporated.

Piped natural gas tax. On a quarterly basis, the state distributes to each city and town served by a natural gas system one-half of the tax proceeds of its excise tax on the distribution of piped natural gas attributable to the sales made within the city or town. There are no special eligibility requirements to receive the funds, and a town may use its piped natural gas tax proceeds to fund any activity in which a town is authorized to engage.

A town should receive its first quarterly share of the piped natural gas tax proceeds within seventy-five days of the end of the first calendar quarter after it is incorporated.

Video Programming Services Taxes. As of January 1, 2007, all cities, towns, and counties will receive, in place of local cable franchise taxes, a quarterly distribution of their share of revenues from three state sales taxes: 7.23 percent of the net proceeds of tax collections on telecommunications services, 22.61 percent of the net proceeds of taxes collected on video programming services, and 37 percent of the net proceeds of taxes collected on direct-to-home satellite services.

A portion of this money is distributed to local governments to support local public, educational, or government access channels. The remaining funds are distributed to cities, towns, and counties according to a formula based, in part, on whether the local government imposed a cable franchise tax on July 1, 2006; the formula is adjusted each year to reflect relative changes in local populations. Newly incorporated towns will share in the proceeds allocated to the county on a per capita basis.

To receive the video programming services taxes proceeds, a town must meet the same eligibility requirements as it does to receive local sales and use tax proceeds. A newly incorporated town may use its video programming services taxes proceeds to fund any activity in which a town is authorized to engage.

If a town is incorporated before the state's annual estimate of population is certified by the state budget officer (usually in late August or early September), it should receive its first quarterly share of the video programming services tax proceeds within seventy-five days of the end of the first quarter after its incorporation. If it is incorporated after the annual certification occurs, it may not receive its first allocation until seventy-five days following the end of the first quarter in which its population is included in the certified annual estimate.

Beer and wine taxes. The state shares with cities, towns, and counties 23.75 percent of its excise tax on beer, 62 percent of its excise tax on unfortified wine, and 22 percent of its excise tax on fortified wine. The annual distribution of the beer and wine tax revenue to local governments is based on the population of eligible units.

A town is eligible to share in beer or wine excise tax revenues if it is legal to sell beer or wine within its boundaries. If only one beverage may be sold, the town shares only in the tax proceeds for that beverage. A town may use its beer and wine tax proceeds to fund any activity in which a town is authorized to engage.

If a town is incorporated before the state's annual estimate of population is certified by the state budget officer (usually in late August or early September), it should receive its first annual allocation of beer and wine taxes revenue within sixty days of the end of the first March in which it is incorporated. The allocation will be based on beer and wine tax proceeds from the preceding twelve-month period. If the town is incorporated after the annual certification occurs, it probably will not receive its first allocation until sixty days following the end of the second March after it is incorporated.

Telecommunications tax. The state levies a sales tax on the gross receipts of telecommunications services and shares a portion of the proceeds from this tax with cities and towns. The proceeds are in addition to the share of telecommunications services taxes shared with local governments for video programming services. The total amount that is distributed to cities and towns each quarter is 18.03 percent of the tax proceeds from that quarter minus $2.6 million. Newly incorporated towns receive a per capita share of the portion of the total to be distributed to all towns incorporated after January 1, 2001. The portion distributed to these towns is calculated by dividing the population of the towns incorporated on or after January 1, 2001, by the population of all cities and counties in the state and multiplying by the total amount to be distributed.

To receive the telecommunications tax proceeds, a town must meet the same eligibility requirements as it does to receive local sales and use tax proceeds. A town can use its telecommunications tax proceeds to fund any activity in which a town is authorized to engage.

If a town is incorporated before the state's annual estimate of population is certified by the state budget officer (usually in late August or early September), it should receive its first quarterly share of the telecommunications tax proceeds within seventy-five days of the end of the first quarter after its incorporation. If it is incorporated after the annual certification occurs, it is not likely to receive its first allocation until seventy-five days after the end of the first quarter in which its population is included in the certified annual estimate.

Miscellaneous Revenue

ABC revenue. Local alcoholic beverage control (ABC) systems normally operate at a profit, and that profit is distributed to local governments. If a system is operated by the county, the general law of North Carolina provides that all profits go to the county government. However, special legislation enacted for particular towns or counties provides that part of the profits of those county systems be distributed to towns within the county. Therefore, a new town located in a county to which the special legislation applies may receive a share of ABC profits.

In addition, a town in a dry county that has at least 500 registered voters may hold an ABC election. If the election succeeds and an ABC system is established, all profits will go to the town.

Projecting Revenues for a New Town

The preceding section identifies the principal revenue sources available to a newly incorporated town. But how can a community estimate how much revenue it can expect to receive from each revenue source? This is an important question—the answer to which is not easy to generalize. There is likely to be significant variation among communities, based on factors such as population, geographic location, number of public streets, value of real estate, access to utilities, amount of commercial activity, and level of services desired by residents of the community.

There are, however, a number of resources available to help a community estimate the revenues it is likely to receive as a newly incorporated town. The North Carolina Department of Revenue (NCDOR) gathers yearly financial statistics on locally raised and county- and state-shared revenues for each city, town, and county in the state.[5] Additionally, the department uses yearly data on municipal revenues and expenditures to compile summary statistics and prepare comparative charts and graphs for various population categories.[6] It also prepares specific reports on state- and county-shared revenues.[7]

Yearly reports on Powell Bill funds are also prepared by the NCDOT; they detail the amount of revenue distributed to each city and town as well as the per capita rate and the rates per street mile. These reports are available on NCDOT's website.[8]

Perhaps the best way to project potential revenues is to contact other North Carolina towns of similar size that supply the number or level of town services the community plans to provide. The NCDOR lists the cities and towns that fall within each population category, along with its summary statistics. *Community leaders looking at these statistics as possible models need to keep in mind that towns incorporated prior to January 1, 2000, do not have to meet many of the eligibility requirements that towns incorporated after that date must satisfy.*

Sample Budgets

The remainder of this chapter sets out sample budgets for three towns, each one preceded by a description of the assumptions on which it is based. The first two budgets are for towns of different population levels. The third is an example of a town that provides the bare minimum of services and charges the lowest possible tax rate needed to qualify for county- and state-shared revenues. Two preliminary comments are in order.

---

5 This data is available at http://www.treasurer.state.nc.us/lgc/units/aboutm.htm (last visited 10 May 2007).

6. Available at http://ncdst-web2.treasurer.state.nc.us/lgc/units/unitlistjs.htm (last visited 20 June 2007).

7. http://www.dor.state.nc.us/publications/reimbursement.html (last visited 20 June 2007).

8. At http://www.ncdot.org/financial/fiscal/ExtAuditBranch/Powell_Bill/powellbill.html (last visited 20 June 2007).

First, the budgets represented are for established towns, not brand-new ones. A newly incorporated town probably will have a somewhat smaller operating budget. The purpose of presenting the sample budgets is to illustrate the financial implications of incorporation over the long run.

Second, although the hypothetical towns for which these budgets are drawn are small, they are representative of independent urban communities; they include both residential and business districts and have one or more industrial plants located either within their boundaries or nearby. None of these budgets is typical of one for either a resort community or a residential suburb of a large city.

Sample 1: Budget for a Town of 1,000 Population

Assumptions. The town was incorporated in 2001 and comprises a small urban community in the southeastern part of the state. It originally had 500 residents, but since incorporation both population growth within the original territorial boundaries and the 2004 annexation of a residential subdivision have doubled the number of residents.

The titles and salaries of the town's four full-time employees and one part-time employee are as follows:

- town administrator/town clerk/budget officer, $57,360
- deputy town clerk (part-time), $9,324
- tax collector, $36,500
- finance officer, $42,380
- enforcement officer, $34,456

Fringe benefits for full-time employees are calculated at 18 percent of salary.

The town's governing board consists of four councilmen and a mayor. The councilmen are paid a yearly salary of $500 each, and the mayor receives $1,000.

The town offers several services to its residents—most of which are provided under contract by the state, county, or a private entity. It contracts with the county sheriff's office to provide additional police protection to town residents. It also contracts with the county to perform building inspections; the county charges regulatory inspection fees to the town's citizens to pay for the inspection services. The town contracts with the state to provide street maintenance services and uses its Powell Bill funds, augmented by General Fund revenue, to reimburse the state. And it contracts with a private electric company to install and maintain street lighting. The town regulates zoning internally; it employs one zoning enforcement officer and has a five-member board of adjustment to review any challenges to the enforcement officer's decisions. It charges various permit fees to offset much of the costs involved in zoning. Finally, the town offers various summer camp and sports league recreational activities—the costs of which are supported mainly by user fees.

The town owns one car, two tractors, and a pickup truck. It intends to purchase an additional tractor this fiscal year.

The town used to own and operate a sewer management system, but it sold it to the county in 2005. It does not currently provide any public enterprise services. Residents receive water and sewer services from the county and other enterprise services from private companies.

The town's assessed valuation is $118,488,443, and its tax rate is 25 cents per $100 valuation. It has a 96 percent collection rate. It currently has no outstanding debt obligations.

Budget 1

Appropriations			Revenues		
General Fund			*General Fund*		
General Government			*Ad valorem Taxes*		
Council and clerk salaries and employee benefits	$13,070		Taxes	$289,797	
Professional services	$19,260		Penalties and interest	$1,923	
Membership dues	$1,158				
Other operating expenses	$45,451		*Other Taxes and Licenses*		
			Privilege license taxes	$7,653	
Administration					
Salaries and employee benefits	$160,763		*Unrestricted Intergovernmental*		
Other administrative costs	$104,358		Local option sales and use taxes	$106,755	
Capital outlay	$14,699		State franchise taxes	$25,384	
			Beer and wine tax	$1,886	
Planning and Zoning			ABC profit	$113,466	
Salaries and employee benefits	$40,658		Video programming services taxes	$4,900	
Legal	$30,691				
Contract services	$33,282		*Restricted Intergovernmental*		
Other operating expenses	$21,975		Powell Bill funds	$32,187	
Public Safety			*Permits and Fees*		
Police protection	$52,000		Building permits	$8,640	
			Recreation fees	$39,000	
Transportation					
Street lights	$17,528		*Investment Earnings*	$15,073	
Street maintenance	$47,350				
			Miscellaneous	$500	
Public Buildings					
Rental	$19,921				
Contingency	$25,000				
Total Expenditures	**$647,164**		**Total Revenues**	**$647,164**	

Sample 2: Budget for a Village of 2,500 Population

Assumptions. The village was incorporated in 2002 and is located in the western part of the state.

The following is a list of its current employees and their yearly salaries:

- town manager/budget officer, $44,000
- town clerk/finance officer, $32,010
- assistant town clerk/tax collector (part-time), $9,000
- five full-time law enforcement officers, $34,326 (avg.)
- zoning administrator, $42,000
- utilities supervisor, $64,650
- two utilities maintenance workers, $25,800 (avg.)

The village offers its employees an attractive array of benefits, calculated at 30 percent of salary for non–law enforcement personnel and 35 percent of salary for law enforcement personnel.

The village has an elected mayor, who receives a yearly stipend of $2,600, and five elected councilmen, who each receive $2,000 per year. In addition, the village reimburses governing board members for certain training and travel expenses.

The village offers its citizens a number of services, including police protection, zoning, water, street maintenance, and street lighting. It contracts with the state to maintain its streets and pays the state with a combination of Powell Bill and General Fund monies. It contracts with private contractors to maintain the street lighting and with the county to perform building inspections; the county retains the fees associated with inspections as reimbursement. The village is located in a rural fire protection district, and residents pay a special fire district tax—collected by the county—to support a volunteer fire department. The village makes a yearly contribution to the volunteer fire department to cover small equipment purchases, and it provides the funding for one fire truck, which it leases to the department.

The village owns and operates its own water supply system. It charges customers tiered user rates, whereby the rates increase with increased usage. The monthly minimum fee for customers who reside in the village is $11.25, which covers up to 2,000 gallons of usage. It also charges a water tap-on fee of $400 per meter to new customers and a $1,000 impact fee on all new development. The village serves several customers who reside outside its corporate limits and charges them double the rate charged residents of the village. The village also contracts with a private firm to provide solid waste collection service, for which it assesses a monthly fee of $11.00 per refuse cart. Other public enterprise services—such as sewer service, electricity, and natural gas—are provided by the county or by private entities.

The village's assessed valuation is $92,927,842, and its tax rate is 48 cents per $100 valuation. It has a 98 percent collection rate. This year the village expects to receive a $20,000 matching grant from the U.S. Department of Homeland Security to upgrade its law enforcement communications system. The only village debt is a Drinking Water State Revolving Fund loan to the public enterprise water fund, used to upgrade a water tank. Annual debt service is $23,000.

Budget 2

Appropriations		Revenues	
General Fund		**General Fund**	
Administration		*Local Revenue*	
Governing board stipend and benefits	$12,600	Ad valorem tax, current year	$440,605
		Ad valorem tax, prior year	$34,500
Governing board training and travel	$3,000	Motor vehicle license tax	$7,500
		Privilege license fees	$1,483
Full-time salaries and benefits	$108,586	Animal tax	$3,329
Part-time salaries and wages	$9,000		
Utilities	$6,900	*Local Fees*	
Staff training and travel	$4,000	Recreation fees	$132,000
Office supplies and marketing	$18,800	Solid waste collection fees	$124,000
Service contracts	$18,000	Miscellaneous fees	$2,660
Insurance and bonding	$10,000	Planning and zoning fees	$56,700
Dues and memberships	$3,000		
Local sales and use taxes	$342,000	*County- and State-Shared Revenue*	
Community support	$6,150	Local sales and use taxes	$342,000
Water billing contract	$5,000	Powell Bill funds	$71,000
Audit services	$8,000	Electric franchise and telecommunication taxes	$69,179
Bank charges	$500		
Elections	$1,350	Video programming services taxes	$5,000
		Beer and wine taxes	$9,800
Planning and Zoning		ABC revenue	$250
Salaries and benefits	$54,600		
Legal fees	$30,691	*Miscellaneous Revenue*	
Other operating expenditures	$51,975	N.C. sales tax refund	$16,302
		Sale of assets	$2,000
Fire Services		Law enforcement matching grant	$20,000
Supplies	$21,500	County recreation contribution	$2,000
Capital outlay	$10,000	Investment income	$12,340
Vehicle lease-purchase	$26,000		
Public Buildings, Grounds, and Equipment			
Cemetery	$1,000		
Maintenance /landscaping	$60,000		
Capital outlay	$2,805		

Budget 2 (*continued*)

Appropriations		Revenues	
General Fund		*General Fund*	
Law Enforcement			
Salaries and benefits	$264,046		
Training	$2,500		
Utilities	$6,400		
Supplies	$18,800		
Communications	$3,000		
Uniforms	$5,000		
Capital outlay/grant match	$41,800		
Streets			
Street maintenance	$62,345		
Street lighting maintenance	$12,000		
Solid Waste Services			
Garbage/recycling/yard waste collection	$142,300		
Recreation			
Leagues	$52,000		
Seasonal programming	$110,000		
Supplies	$96,000		
Contingency	$63,000		
Total General Expenditures	**$1,352,648**	**Total General Revenues**	**$1,352,648**

continued on page 40

Budget 2 (continued)

Appropriations		Revenues	

Enterprise Funds

Water Fund

Salaries and benefits	$151,525		
Utilities	$18,000		
Water analysis	$3,000		
Water tank maintenance	$28,630		
Water meter program	$15,000		
Training and travel	$5,000		
Supplies /uniforms	$18,900		
Dues	$1,000		
Capital outlay	$9,000		
Debt service for water tank upgrade	$23,000		

Enterprise Funds

Water Fund

Water use charges	$244,455
Water connect fee	$2,400
Water impact fees	$5,000
Penalties	$18,000
Interest income	$3,200

Total Water Expenditures	**$273,055**	**Total Water Revenues**	**$273,055**

Sample 3: Budget for Town Providing Minimum Services at Minimum Tax Rate

Assumptions: The town was incorporated on July 1, 2002, to avoid annexation by a neighboring city. It has approximately 2,000 residents and is located approximately thirty miles outside a major city.

The town has four full-time employees with the following yearly salaries:

- planning and zoning director, $48,000
- permit specialist/administrative assistant, $25,000
- zoning administrator, $33,500
- clerk/finance officer ($35,000)

Fringe benefits for all employees are calculated at 20 percent of salary.

The town also has five councilmen and a mayor. Council members each receive an annual salary of $150, and the mayor receives $250.

The town provides four basic services—zoning, solid waste collection, police protection, and street maintenance. It contracts with other governments and private entities to perform most of these services. It also contracts with the county sheriff's department to provide additional police services to town residents. The state maintains the town's streets and is paid with the town's Powell Bill allocation. A private hauler handles garbage collection through an agreement with the town. Although user fees cover most of the garbage collection expenses, the town subsidizes the fee proceeds with some General Fund revenue. In addition, the county performs building inspections, keeping the inspection fees as reimbursement.

Aside from solid waste collection, the town provides no public enterprise services to residents. Water, sewer, electric, natural gas, and cable services all are provided by private companies. The town is located in a rural fire protection district, and its citizens pay an additional district tax to fund the services of a volunteer fire department. The town makes a yearly contribution to the fire department to cover some of its costs.

The town's assessed valuation is $4,903,920. The tax rate is 5 cents per $100 valuation, and the anticipated collection percentage is about 98 percent. It currently has no outstanding debt obligations. During the current fiscal year the town entered into an agreement to purchase five acres of open land with General Fund proceeds.

Budget 3

Appropriations		Revenues	
General Fund		**General Fund**	
Administration		*Sources*	
Salaries and related expenses	$170,800	Ad valorem taxes	$250,200
Professional services	$36,300	Sales and use taxes	$68,400
Office expenses	$20,694	Motor vehicle taxes	$14,800
Furnishings and equipment	$10,000	Beer and wine taxes	$8,000
Training and travel	$3,000	Electric, natural gas, and	$69,400
Dues and subscriptions	$3,132	telecommunications taxes	
Community events	$2,700	Park land fees	$19,500
Elections	$600	Zoning fees	$62,500
Land acquisition	$51,586	Powell Bill allocation	$54,430
Contingency	$24,000	Video programming services tax	$4,000
		Interest and miscellaneous	$5,460
	$322,812		**$556,690**
Zoning	**$75,987**		
Public Safety			
Police	$62,501		
Fire	$7,500		
	$70,001		
Streets/Sanitation			
Street maintenance	$54,430		
Solid waste collection	$8,000		
	$62,430		
Nondepartmental			
Insurance	$7,350		
Town Hall rent	$18,110		
	$25,460		
Total Expenditures	**$556,690**	**Total Revenues**	**$556,690**

6. Starting Up a New Town

Town Finances

A recurring problem for newly incorporated towns—and one with no ready solution—is providing money to operate during the town's first few months of existence. As indicated by the discussion of town revenues in Chapter 5, "Financing a Town," proceeds from the major sources of revenue do not begin to arrive until several months after incorporation. Until then, financing the town's operations can be difficult. There are a number of possible ways to cover expenses during this interim period.

1. Some suppliers of goods and services may be willing to wait a few months to be paid—particularly if they see prospects for future business once revenue collections are regularized.

2. Some persons or business firms that owe large property tax bills might pay them early as a favor to the town. The town can encourage this practice by offering discounts for early payment. (A discount schedule must be adopted by the town by the May 1 before the first fiscal year for which it is applicable and then be approved by the state Department of Revenue.)

3. A town can borrow in anticipation of later revenues. It may not, however, simply go to a local bank and borrow the money. Such a loan is subject to a variety of limitations and must be approved by the Local Government Commission, an agency within the Department of the State Treasurer. If a town wants to investigate this step, it should get in touch with the treasurer's office at the earliest possible date.

4. The town can delay providing town services for a few months—until revenues begin to flow.

Other Start-Up Steps

1. New town officials should notify county tax officials of the town's existence and its boundaries. The county tax assessor will then calculate the tax base and notify the town government. Either the town or the county—depending on which will collect town taxes—will prepare tax collection records.

2. The town needs to decide whether to join the Social Security system (almost all towns do) and the state-administered Local Government Employees' Retirement System. Information pertinent to both decisions is available from the Retirement Systems Division of the Office of the State Treasurer.

3. If the area within the new town has been subject to county zoning, the county's zoning regulations expire no later than sixty days after the effective date of incorporation. The new town therefore needs to act quickly to put its own zoning in place. The county planning department may be available to help town officials with this process.

4. If no incorporation election was held, the town should notify the county board of elections of the town's existence and boundaries and make payment arrangements for the board's conduct of town elections.

5. To receive state street aid (Powell Bill funds), the town must engage an engineer or a surveyor to survey and map the town's streets. The town should also reach agreement with the district engineer of the N.C. Department of Transportation (DOT) about the state–town division of responsibility for maintenance of public streets and highways within the town.

6. The town should contact the Government Records branch of the Department of Cultural Resources and sign a contract agreeing to observe the state's schedule for retention and disposition of records. From the outset, the town should be precise in establishing and maintaining town records, particularly financial records and minutes of town and board meetings. The Government Records branch can help town officials establish a general records system, and the State and Local Government Finance Division of the Office of the State Treasurer can provide assistance in establishing financial records. The certified public accountant engaged to perform the town's annual audit can also be helpful with this task.

Matters for the First Governing Board

1. The initial act of the town's first governing board must be an organizational meeting at which the new officials are sworn into office and the mayor pro tempore is elected from among board members. If the mayor, as well as the mayor pro tempore, is to be chosen by the board, that election takes place at the same meeting. Oaths of office may be administered by any justice, judge, or magistrate or retired judges and justices; by the clerk, deputy clerk, or assistant clerk of superior court in the county; by any notary public; by the register of deeds; by the chair of the board of county commissioners; by a legislator; by a city clerk or clerk to the board of county commissioners; or by any mayor (including the town's new mayor after he or she is sworn in). Appointment of a town clerk and a town attorney should also take place at this meeting. Often, the attorney who helped with the incorporation effort becomes the town attorney. Finally, the new governing board establishes a schedule of regular meeting days and times.

2. The board members should be made aware of the limitations on their legal ability to contract with the town in their private business capacities. Only in towns of less than 15,000 population may a board member conduct private business with the town; even in those small towns the maximum allowable amount of such business in any one year is $25,000. A violation of the rules mentioned in this paragraph constitutes a misdemeanor for the offending board member and renders void any contract illegally entered into between the board member and the town. Even when such transactions are permitted, a number of procedural requirements must be met. For all of these reasons, board members should consult with the town attorney whenever the possibility of selling goods or services to the town arises.

Sources of Assistance

The same agencies that can help a community that is studying incorporation—the School of Government, the North Carolina League of Municipalities, and the local councils of governments—can also assist a new town in beginning operations. In addition, officials of nearby towns or of other recently incorporated towns are often invaluable sources of information.

Appendix A

Government Structures and Election Methods of North Carolina Municipalities, by Population

	23 cities over 25,000	39 cities 10,000– 25,000	45 cities 5,000– 10,000	86 cities 2,500– 5,000	118 cities 1,000– 2,500	99 cities 500– 1,000	139 cities under 500	549 cities Total
Style of Corporation								
City	21	19	18	6	3	3	0	70
Town	2	19	26	78	111	94	129	459
Village	0	1	1	2	4	2	10	20
Style of Governing Board								
Board of Commissioners	0	8	13	38	72	62	92	285
Board of Aldermen	2	4	4	14	17	14	16	71
Council	21	27	28	34	29	23	31	193
Form of Government								
Council–Manager	23	37	40	59	42	11	8	220
Mayor–Council	0	2	5	27	76	88	131	329
Selection of Mayor								
Mayor elected by the people	22	39	43	81	113	87	125	510
Mayor selected by and from governing board	1	0	2	5	5	11	11	35
Other	0	0	0	0	0	1	3	4

continued on page 48

Government Structures and Election Methods of North Carolina
Municipalities, by Population (continued)

	23 cities over 25,000	39 cities 10,000– 25,000	45 cities 5,000– 10,000	86 cities 2,500– 5,000	118 cities 1,000– 2,500	99 cities 500– 1,000	139 cities under 500	549 cities Total
Mayor's Term of Office								
2 years	14	19	27	36	65	58	106	325
4 years	9	20	17	45	51	35	29	206
At board's pleasure	0	0	1	5	2	6	4	18
No. on Governing Board								
11	1	0	0	0	0	0	0	1
9	1	0	0	0	0	0	0	1
8	4	6	1	0	0	0	0	11
7	4	7	3	1	1	1	0	17
6	11	7	7	15	11	2	2	55
5	1	13	25	49	77	70	77	312
4	1	6	9	20	27	20	28	111
3	0	0	0	1	2	6	31	40
2	0	0	0	0	0	0	1	1
Governing Board Term of Office								
2 years	10	9	8	15	22	35	81	180
4 years	3	1	3	2	3	6	10	28
Staggered 4-year terms	10	27	33	67	93	56	46	332
Other	0	2	1	2	0	2	2	9

continued on page 49

Government Structures and Election Methods of North Carolina Municipalities, by Population (continued)

	23 cities over 25,000	39 cities 10,000– 25,000	45 cities 5,000– 10,000	86 cities 2,500– 5,000	118 cities 1,000– 2,500	99 cities 500– 1,000	139 cities under 500	549 cities Total
Mode of Election								
At large	7	21	30	73	108	96	137	472
At large, with district residence requirement	2	3	6	7	3	1	2	24
Combination of at-large members and members elected at large but representing districts	2	0	3	1	1	1	0	8
Elected by & from districts	5	5	2	2	3	1	0	18
Combination of at-large and district members	7	10	4	3	3	0	0	27
Type of Election								
Partisan elections	2	2	1	3	1	0	0	9
Nonpartisan primary	8	5	2	5	3	2	0	25
Election determined by majority of votes cast, with runoff	5	7	5	3	2	5	1	28
Election decided by plurality	8	25	37	75	112	92	138	487

Appendix B

Charter of the Town of Boroughville

Chapter I

Incorporation and Corporate Powers

§ 1-1. **Incorporation and corporate powers.** The inhabitants of the Town of Boroughville are a body corporate and politic under the name "Town of Boroughville." Under that name they have all the powers, duties, rights, privileges, and immunities conferred and imposed on cities by the general law of North Carolina.

[*Comment:* This chapter simply states the corporate existence of the city and gives it all the powers of cities under North Carolina law.]

Chapter II

Corporate Boundaries

Article 1. Town Boundaries

§ 2-1. **Town boundaries.** Until modified in accordance with law, the boundaries of the Town of Boroughville are as follows: [Describe boundaries.]

Article 2. Electoral District Boundaries

§ 2-5. **Electoral district boundaries.** Until modified in accordance with law, the boundaries of the electoral districts of the Town of Boroughville are as follows: [Describe the district boundaries.]

[*Comment:* If a town is divided into districts (or wards) for purposes of electing the governing board, this section would be the appropriate place in the charter to refer to the boundaries of those districts.]

Chapter III

Governing Body

§ 3-1. **Structure of governing body; number of members.**

[Choose one of two]

[A] The governing body of the Town of Boroughville is the Board of Aldermen, which has five members, and the Mayor.

OR

[B] The governing body of the Town of Boroughville is the Board of Aldermen, which has five members.

§ 3-2. **Manner of electing Board.**

[Choose one of four]

[A] The qualified voters of the entire Town [nominate and] elect the members of the Board.

OR

[B] The Town is divided into five electoral districts. The qualified voters of each district [nominate and] elect one member of the Board. To be eligible for [nomination and] election to the Board from a district and for service on the Board as member for a district, a person must reside in the district.

OR

[C] The Town is divided into five electoral districts. The qualified voters of each district nominate persons for one seat on the Board, and the qualified voters of the entire Town elect the members of the Board. To be eligible for nomination and election to the Board from a district and for service on the Board as member for a district, a person must reside in the district.

OR

[D] The Town is divided into five electoral districts, and each district is represented on the Board by one member. The qualified voters of the entire Town [nominate and] elect the members of the Board. To be eligible for [nomination and] election to the Board and for service on the Board as member for a district, a person must reside in the district.

§ 3-3. **Term of office of Board members.**

[Choose one of two]

[A] Members of the Board are elected to two-year terms.

OR

[B] Members of the Board are elected to four-year terms. In [2007] and each four years thereafter, two members of the Board shall be elected. In [2009] and each four years thereafter, three members of the Board shall be elected.

§ 3-4. **Election of Mayor; term of office.**

[Choose one of two]

[A] The qualified voters of the entire Town elect the Mayor. He or she is elected to a two-year term of office.

OR

[B] At the organizational meeting of the Board following each election, the Board shall elect one of its members to serve as Mayor. The Mayor shall serve as such at the pleasure of the Board.

[*Comment:* This chapter of the charter provides for those details of governing board structure that will differ from city to city and must therefore be provided for by charter. It names the governing board, provides for its size, specifies the manner of election of its members and the length of their terms, and provides for the method of electing the mayor. A discussion of each of the sections follows.]

Section 3-1. This section establishes the basic structure of the governing body. The two alternatives differ with regard to how the mayor is elected. If the mayor is elected separately by the voters, the mayor and the governing board constitute the governing body; this is alternative A. If the mayor is elected by and from the governing board, the mayor remains a member of that board, and the governing board is the governing body; this is alternative B.

Whichever alternative is selected, this section will specify the name of the governing board and the number of its members. The number, of course, can be anything, and the board might just as well be called the "Board of Commissioners" or the "Council" as the "Board of Aldermen."

Section 3-2. This section specifies whether board members are to be elected at large or from electoral districts (or wards). The four options embody the four basic possibilities:

   A. No districts, with all members elected at large.
   B. Districts, with all members elected from districts.
   C. Districts, with all members nominated by district voters but elected at large.
   D. Districts, with all members required to reside in districts but elected at large.

Draft options A, B, and D all contain language in brackets that pertains to the nomination process. Whether the bracketed language will be included in a particular charter depends on whether that city will hold primary elections.

These four basic election options can be modified. A governing board might have some members elected at large and others from districts; or some of the districts might be represented by more than one member. Space does not allow for the setting out of each possible modification.

Section 3-3. This section specifies the length of governing board terms and presents two alternatives. In alternative A all members serve two-year terms; in alternative B all members serve four-year terms and the terms are staggered. (The four-year terms need not be staggered.)

If a city uses electoral districts and the members of its governing board serve staggered terms, this section should specify which district seats are to be filled in which years. If both are simple, sections 3-3 and 3-2 could easily be combined.

Section 3-4. This section details how the mayor is elected; the choice of alternative provisions should parallel that made for section 3-1. Alternative A provides for a mayor elected directly by the voters and should be used with alternative A of section 3-1. Alternative B provides for a mayor elected by and from the governing board and should be used with alternative B of section 3-1.

Within each alternative presented, the mayor's term of office can be varied. Many mayors elected directly by the voters are elected for four-year terms. (The mayor's term need not be the same length as that of the governing board members.) Some mayors elected by their governing boards serve established terms of one or two years.

Chapter IV

Elections

§ 4-1. **Conduct of town elections.**

[Choose one of four]

[A] Town officers shall be nominated and elected on a partisan basis, as provided by G.S. 163-291.

OR

[B] Town officers shall be elected on a nonpartisan basis and the results determined by a plurality of votes cast, as provided by G.S. 163-292.

OR

[C] Town officers shall be elected on a nonpartisan basis and the results determined by a majority of votes cast, with a runoff election if necessary, as provided by G.S. 163-293.

OR

[D] Town officers shall be nominated in a primary and elected on a nonpartisan basis, as provided by G.S. 163-294.

[*Comment:* Since there is a uniform Municipal Election Law, a charter need only specify the city's choice among the four optional methods of conducting city elections. The four options presented each embody one of the methods, and each contains the appropriate citations.]

Chapter V

Administration

§ 5-1.

[Choose one of two]

Town to operate under council-manager plan. The Town of Boroughville operates under the council-manager plan as provided in G.S. Chapter 160A, Article 7, Part 2.

OR

Town to operate under mayor-council plan. The Town of Boroughville operates under the mayor-council plan as provided in G.S. Chapter 160A, Article 7, Part 3.

[*Comment:* The two possibilities presented represent a town's decision on whether to have a manager. Whatever the decision, the section will state it and then simply refer to the general law, which contains the necessary legal framework.]